We Love Electric Cars

Katherine Lewis

BUMBA BOOKS™

LERNER PUBLICATIONS ◆ MINNEAPOLIS

Note to Educators

Throughout this book, you'll find critical-thinking questions. These can be used to engage young readers in thinking critically about the topic and in using the text and photos to do so.

For McKenzie

Lerner Publications Company
An imprint of Lerner Publishing Group, Inc.
241 First Avenue North
Minneapolis, MN 55401 USA

For reading levels and more information, look up this title at www.lernerbooks.com.

Main body text set in Helvetica Textbook Com.
Typeface provided by Linotype AG.

Library of Congress Cataloging-in-Publication Data

Names: Lewis, Katherine, 1996– author.
Title: We love electric cars / Katherine Lewis.
Description: Minneapolis : Lerner Publications, [2021] | Series: Bumba books - we love cars and trucks | Includes bibliographical references and index. | Audience: Ages 4–7 | Audience: Grades K–1 | Summary: "Quiet and rechargeable, electric cars are becoming more popular. Readers will love learning about these energy-saving cars and discovering what makes them different from other rides"— Provided by publisher.
Identifiers: LCCN 2020014646 (print) | LCCN 2020014647 (ebook) | ISBN 9781728419251 (library binding) | ISBN 9781728420301 (paperback) | ISBN 9781728419299 (ebook)
Subjects: LCSH: Electric automobiles—Juvenile literature.
Classification: LCC TL220 .L49 2021 (print) | LCC TL220 (ebook) | DDC 629.22/93—dc23

LC record available at https://lccn.loc.gov/2020014646
LC ebook record available at https://lccn.loc.gov/2020014647

Manufactured in the United States of America
1-49041-49257-6/17/2020

Table of Contents

Electric Cars

Electric cars have motors instead of engines. Motors are powered by electricity, not gas.

Burning gas for energy

makes clouds of dirty smoke.

Electricity is cleaner and

healthier!

Batteries power electric motors. The batteries are charged with electricity.

What do you think happens when the batteries run out of energy?

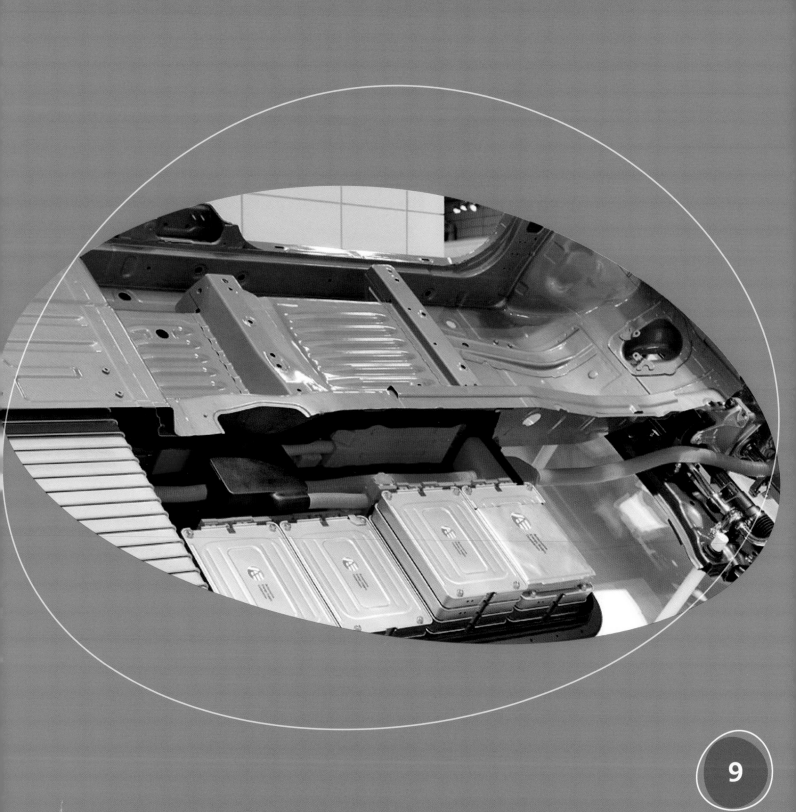

Drivers must charge the battery.

Drivers can do this at home.

They can also go to a charging station.

Where might you find a charging station?

Electric cars come in many colors.

They come in many sizes too!

Some electric cars are very fast. Teslas are popular electric cars.

Some cars have both electric motors and gas engines.

These cars are called hybrids.

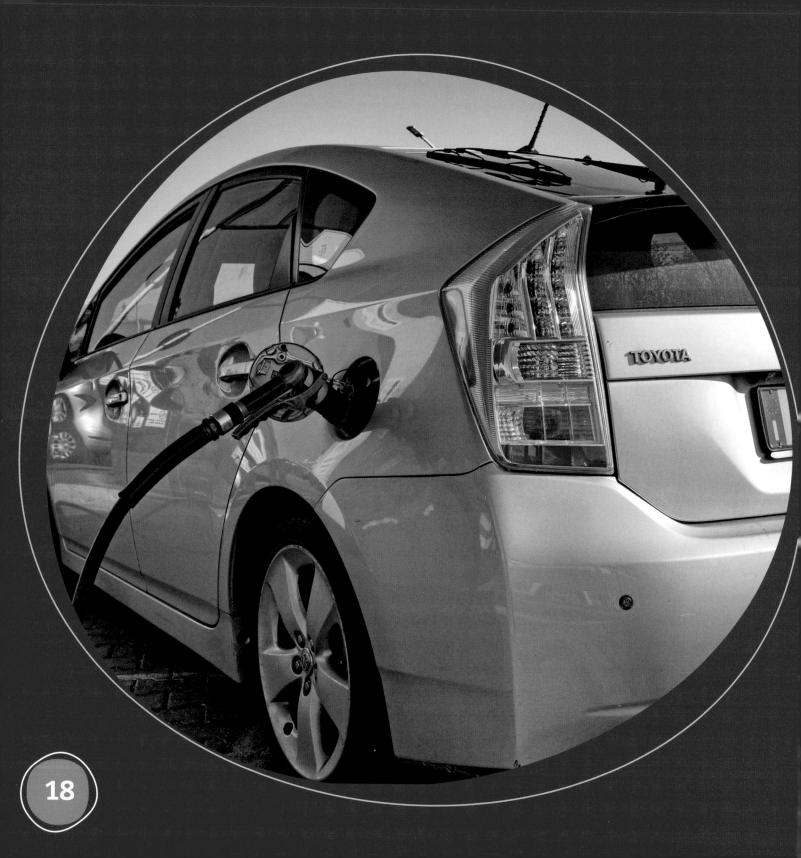

Hybrid cars use both

gas and electricity.

Many people like

hybrid cars.

More and more people
are buying electric cars.
Would you like to drive
one someday?

Why might electric cars become more popular?

Parts of an Electric Car

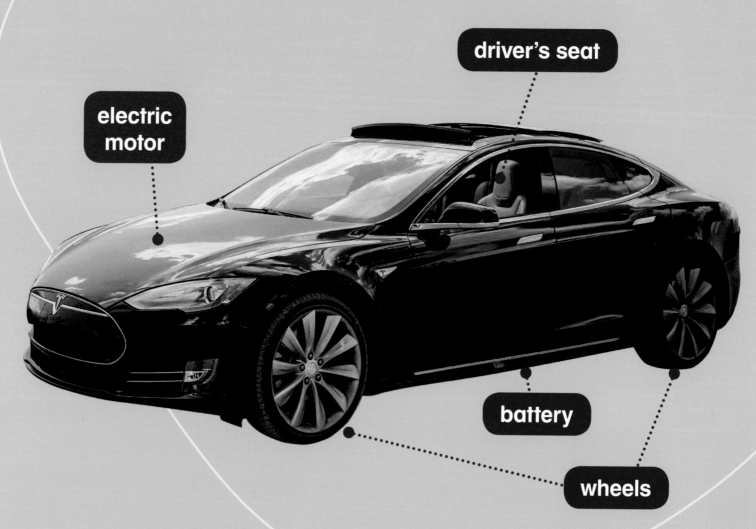

driver's seat

electric motor

battery

wheels

Picture Glossary

battery

a tool that stores energy to power machines

charging station

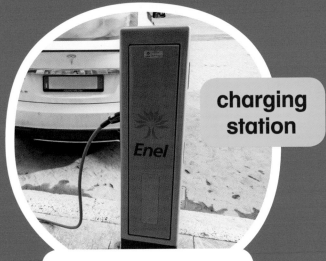

a place to charge electric cars

electric motor

a machine that powers electric cars

hybrid

a car that uses gas and electricity

23

Learn More

Levit, Joe. *Let's Explore Technology*. Minneapolis: Lerner Publications, 2019.

Murray, Julie. *Tesla Model S*. Minneapolis: Abdo Zoom, 2018.

Pettiford, Rebecca. *Hybrid and Electric Cars*. Minneapolis: Pogo, 2017.

Index

Photo Acknowledgments

Image credits: Joel_420/Shutterstock.com, p. 5; testing/Shutterstock.com, pp. 6–7; Tennen-Gas/Wikimedia Commons (CC BY-SA 3.0), pp. 9, 23 (top right); Evannovostro/Shutterstock.com, pp. 10, 23 (top right); Dmitry Eagle Orlov/Shutterstock.com, p. 13; valentinphotography/Shutterstock.com, pp. 14–15; erkanatbas/Shutterstock.com, pp. 17, 23 (bottom left); assimo Parisi/Shutterstock.com, pp. 18, 23 (bottom right); TierneyMJ/Shutterstock.com, pp. 20–21; valentinphotography/Shutterstock.com, p. 22.

Cover: betto rodrigues/Shutterstock.com.